What If Scriptures

Volume I

By

Thomas R. Long

What If Scriptures, Volume I
Copyright © 2023—Thomas R. Long
ALL RIGHTS RESERVED

Unless otherwise noted, all scripture references are from T*he New King James Version of the Bible*, copyright © 1979, 1980, 1982, by Thomas Nelson, Inc., Nashville, TN. References marked KJV are taken from *The Holy Bible, King James Version*, public domain. References marked NASB are from the New American Standard Bible, copyright © 1960, 1962, 1963, 1968, 1971, 1972, 1973, 1975, 1977 by the Lockman Foundation, La Habra, California. References marked NET are from the *The Holy Bible New English Translation*, copyright ©1996-2017 by Biblical Studies Press, L.L.C. References marked The Interlinear Bible are from *The Interlinear Hebrew-Greek-English Bible*, copyright © 1976, 1977, 1978, 1979, 1980, 1981, 1984 by Jay P. Green Sr. *A Literal Translation of the Bible*, copyright ©1985 by Jay P. Green, Sr., *The Interlinear Greek-English New Testament,* Copyright © 1980, 1981, 1983, 1984 by Jay P. Green Sr. References marked The Aramaic Bible are from *The Holy Aramaic Scriptures*, copyright © 2010-2021 by The Holy Aramaic Scriptures.com. All rights reserved. Used by permission.

Published by:

Tom Long Books
18896 Greenwell Springs Road
Greenwell Springs, LA 70739
www.thepublishedword.com

ISBN: 978-0-9718631-4-9

Printed on demand in the U.S., the U.K., Australia and the EAU
For Worldwide Distribution

Dedication

I want to dedicate this book to my darling wife Nancy, who went with Jesus last year after 52+ years of marriage. She wasn't perfect, but she was perfect for me. She taught me how to love and be a man. Her love of the Lord and constant intercession covered a lot of my issues. Before I met her I had asked the Lord for a woman who loved Him more than I, and I wasn't disappointed.

Nancy was a dreamer in that she was always having dreams. She wrote most of them in notebooks. We worked on their interpretation together.

She also had visions which helped us in numerous ways.

Here is one that she had about 2 years before she died. She was sitting in her office at around 10:00 A.M., when she had this vision.

"I was sitting on a hill playing a musical instrument that I hadn't seen before but knew how to play. The landscape was rolling hills of green grasses. I saw some friends walk by. We said, 'Hello.'

"An angel walked up to me and said, 'Come with me. The King wants to see you.' "How could I refuse?

"We were immediately transported to a magnificent castle overlooking all the land. The angel introduced me to a woman who said she was there to help me with anything I needed and for any concerns I had. She took me into a large reception room toward the top of the castle and we waited. She said it would be just a moment. The room was furnished very nicely, but not too much. The views from the windows were spectacular.

"A little while later the King, Jesus, entered the room with an entourage. He looked in my direction nodded and smiled. He finished His conversation and dismissed the rest, except for the woman assigned to me.

"He came over and sat across from me and we talked for what seemed hours. He answered all my questions. I have never felt such peace and joy.

"There was a knock at the door, an aide entered and said, 'It's time.'

"We finished talking and stood up. He looked at me and said, 'I'll be back.'

"He started toward the door. Then, He stopped, turned around, and came back. He took my hand and repeated, 'I'll be back.'

"I replied, 'I know' and patted Him on the arm." When I did this, I thought, "Nancy, what are you doing? You just patted the King of Kings on the arm. Get a grip." She continued:

"He started to leave and stopped again. He came back and kissed me on the cheek and repeated a third time, 'I'll be back.' Then He left.

"I was in awe of what had happened. The woman asked me if I needed anything. I replied, 'No, I just need to sit a while.'

"A little while later, the angel who brought me returned and said it was time to go. Instantly I was back in my office." This was the end of her vision.

As she told me about this experience, I asked if she remembered what was said. She either couldn't remember or was unwilling to talk about it.

About 2 years later, Nancy suffered an aneurysm bleed in her brain and a stroke, putting her into a coma. I had brought her home after two months in a hospital, still in a coma, to be on hospice care. A week later, I got up early to check her. I left the room for a minute, and when I returned she was gone. I

In that moment I knew He had fulfilled His promise to return for her. This gives me peace.

Father, thank You for Nancy. She was such an incredible gift. Your loving kindness loaned her to me, but she was always Yours.

I also want to thank my friend Nickolas for helping me edit and for his helpful comments.

Contents

Preface 9

1. Puzzling Scripture #1 (Philippians 2:5-11) 13
2. Puzzling Scripture #2 (Genesis 1:1) 31
3. Puzzling Scripture #3 (Isaiah 43:10) 37
4. Puzzling Scripture #4 (Psalm 8) 39
5. Puzzling Scripture #5 (Hebrews 9:27) 47
6. Puzzling Scripture #6 (Genesis 11:1-7) 51
7. Where Is the Throne of God? 55
8. Who Was Melchizedek? 59
9. Puzzling Scripture #7 (John 3:13-17) 63
10. Psalms of Blessing 69
11. YHVH's Story 77

Summary 97

Other Books by Thomas R. Long 102

Preface

This is my fifth book and probably the most controversial. Please read the others before you read this one, especially *The Link*, as the others lay a lot of groundwork that I will not be covering here.

Over the years there have been scriptures that have puzzled me. This last year I felt led to dig into them and seek revelation. This book is about what I have found, what I have concluded, and some of the process I went through. As always, I don't proclaim this as ultimate truth, but rather the results in a search for answers and/or possibilities with the objective of painting a single cohesive picture.

If faced with several possibilities, I have chosen the one that most directly leads to that single picture. If you think I'm using scripture to justify my belief, how am I different from you? When I started this, I had no idea where it would take me, so there was nothing to justify.

Before I get into those puzzling scriptures, I want to lay some ground rules.

First of all, I want to declare that the Bible is not the story of mankind, but the story of the making of the sons of God. If it is the story of mankind, then mankind is the emphasis and not God or His will. If it is the story of the making of the sons of God, then it's all about Him and His will. This also plays into His purpose for creation—offspring.

For scripture references I am using principally the New King James Version of the Bible. References to other versions will be noted as they appear.

Except for scripture, all references to God's names will be portrayed in a way as to not take them in vain.

Genesis 1, while having historic significance, is mainly an allegory about the process of making sons. It is the whole Bible in a single chapter. The rest of the Bible adds history, boundaries, details, and prophecy to this process.

During the writing of this book, I encountered many issues. Some of the traditional translations of the Hebrew words for God and Lord gave me problems as in some places they were translated as proper names and other places as titles. I prayed about this. Here is what I received.

1. Always translate YHVH (Strong's H3068) and Y-H (Strong's H3050) as proper names.
2. For the word Elohiym (Strong's H430):
    a. When the sense is plural, use Elohiym.

What If Scriptures—Vol. 1

   b. When the sense is singular, use god or God when referring to YHVH.
   c. When the sense is unclear, use Elohiym.
   d. When used with a proper name, like YHVH Elohiym, use YHVH (my or our) God.

Last night, I was questioning if I was hearing correctly. I believe the Holy Spirit said, "It is the next step in the process of understanding God and the world. It is a necessary step to the renewing of your mind and becoming an overcomer of the flesh and all the plans of the enemy and to moving forward the formation of the sons of God. For now, it is what is needed. It is by no means complete."

As in all things, ask the Holy Spirit for clarification. It is His job to guide us into all truth. Don't ask if a thing is true, but rather, "Is it for me at this time?" Most of the time I can't handle the truth.

Truth is a point. My understanding of that truth is based upon my perspective. It's like four people viewing an elephant, one on each side. Each believes what he is seeing is true. It is, but not the whole truth. If you believe your perspective is the only one, you are deceived, and all learning has stopped. To gain a new perspective, you must be willing to change and understand that we only know in part (see 1

What If Scriptures—Vol. 1

Corinthians 13:9). It is also impossible for the Holy Spirit to guide you into all truth if you are unwilling to move (see John 16:13). No matter how far you think you've come, there's always more, so much more.

Tom Long

CHAPTER 1

Puzzling Scripture #1

Philippians 2:5-11   Let this mind be in you which was also in Christ Jesus, [6] who, being in the form of God, did not consider it robbery to be equal with God, [7] but made Himself of no reputation, taking the form of a bondservant, *and* coming in the likeness of men. [8] And being found in appearance as a man, He humbled Himself and became obedient to *the point of* death, even the death of the cross.

[9] Therefore God also has highly exalted Him and given Him the name which is above every name, [10] that at the name of Jesus every knee should bow, of those in heaven, and of those on earth, and of those under the earth, [11] and *that* every tongue should confess that Jesus Christ *is* Lord, to the glory of God the Father.

If Jesus is part of the Trinity, i.e., God the Son, then why is a new name necessary? Why aren't heavens mentioned instead of heaven, and why should every tongue confess Him as Lord and not God the Son? Giving Him a new name and only placing Him over Heaven and earth would seem to be a demotion. It doesn't say Jesus was God, but in the form of, like, or with God.

What are the possibilities for this verse being true?

What If Scriptures—Vol. 1

The only possibilities I see is that either God the Son took a demotion or Jesus isn't the Son of the Trinity. God can't cease from being God, so a demotion is out of the question.

How can Jesus not be the Son of the Trinity? That's what I and every other Christian were taught.

This led me on a hunt for other scriptures to validate my new supposition.

Revelations 11:15   Then the seventh angel sounded: And there were loud voices in heaven, saying, "The kingdoms of this world have become *the kingdoms* of <u>our Lord and of His Christ</u>, and He shall reign forever and ever!"

Who is the above scripture referring to as "our Lord"? It can't be Jesus because He is "His Christ." It has to be YHVH.

(I am using YHVH, the Tetragrammaton used in the Old Testament as the name of the God of Abraham, Isaac, and Jacob).

Psalm 2:7   "I will declare the decree:
<u>The LORD [YHVH] has said to Me,</u>
<u>'You are My Son, Today I have begotten You</u>."

What If Scriptures—Vol. 1

In the above scripture, who is "My Son"? Is Jesus not the only begotten Son of God? This verse also begs the question what was the Son the day before He was begotten?

John 3:16   For God so loved the world that He gave <u>His only begotten Son</u>, that whoever believes in Him should not perish but have everlasting life.

The God of John 3:16 is therefore YHVH. If YHVH is the Father of Jesus, is He the Father or the Son of the Trinity?

I find it puzzling that YHVH translated means "Y-H exists." Why would God give Himself a name which translated means Y-H exists unless there is another whose name is Y-H.

Is there a scripture that says this?

Psalm 68:4   Sing to God, sing praises to His name; extol Him who rides on the clouds,
<u>By His name Y</u>AH, and rejoice before Him.

Amazingly, in the King James Bible, the name Y-H (JAH) occurs exactly 49 times (perfection times perfection). It is also part of the universal word "Hallelujah" which means Praise Y-H. The name

What If Scriptures—Vol. 1

Elijah means Y-H is God. It is taught that Y-H is an abbreviation for YHVH.

What if it isn't?

Psalm 94:7   Yet they say, "The LORD [Y-H] does not see, nor does the God of Jacob understand."

In the above verse there are two references to God. If YHVH is the God of Jacob, then who is the Lord? It just so happens that the Hebrew word translated as Lord is Y-H. It appears to me that Y-H and YHVH are two different persons.

In the Hebrew tradition, a son is named after his father. Therefore YHVH's (Y-H exists) father must be Y-H. If Y-H is the Trinity Father, then YHVH is the Trinity Son and Jesus is the only begotten Son of YHVH.

Isaiah 61:1-2   "The Spirit of the Lord GOD *is* upon Me, because the LORD has anointed Me
To preach good tidings to the poor; He has sent Me to heal the brokenhearted,
To proclaim liberty to the captives, and the opening of the prison to *those who are* bound;
² To proclaim the acceptable year of the LORD ... .

What If Scriptures—Vol. 1

In the above verse that Jesus quoted about Himself, it doesn't say He is God, but that the Spirit of YHVH is upon Him, because YHVH has appointed Him. And that Spirit enables and authorizes Him to do these things.

John 14:9   Jesus said to him, "Have I been with you so long, and yet you have not known Me, Philip? He who has seen Me has seen the Father; so how can you say, 'Show us the Father'?

This doesn't say Jesus is the Father, but that by virtue of the Spirit of YHVH being in Him, they were in effect seeing His Father.

John 5:19   Then Jesus answered and said to them, "Most assuredly, I say to you, the Son can do nothing of Himself, but what He sees the Father do; for whatever He does, the Son also does in like manner."

Jesus is saying the same thing here. Because the Spirit of YHVH is upon Me and I only do what He does and say what He says, then you are hearing and seeing the Father by proxy. In modern lingo, Jesus is acting as an avatar for YHVH, but willingly by virtue of His free will.

What If Scriptures—Vol. 1

John 1:18   No one has seen God at any time. The only begotten Son, who is in the bosom of the Father, He has declared *Him.*

Notice in the above verse there are three different persons referenced, God, begotten Son, and Father. I believe it is God (Y-H), begotten Son (Jesus) and Father (YHVH). It appears neither Jesus nor YHVH has seen Y-H, but they testify to His existence.

It does not say that Jesus is the only Son of God, but the only begotten Son (formally declared), He was fully man, with DNA as Adam. Both were genetically engineered by YHVH.

A further question would be: Is YHVH the only begotten Son of Y-H? Does this possibility change your perspective of the above verse?

Job 1:6   Now there was a day when the sons of God [Elohiym] came to present themselves before the LORD [YHVH], and Satan also came among them.

I think it's interesting that the sons of the Elohiym came to present themselves before YHVH.

1 Corinthians 15:22   For as in Adam all die, even so in Christ all shall be made alive.

What If Scriptures—Vol. 1

Since Adam polluted his DNA, divine nature and authority, Jesus was fathered by YHVH with the same or similar DNA as Adam (no sin nature).

1 Corinthians 15:45   And so it is written, "The first man Adam became a living being." <u>The last Adam *became* a life-giving spirit</u>.

If Jesus, the last Adam, became a life-giving spirit, then he wasn't a life-giving spirit (God) to begin with. Because the God-breathed man, Adam, caused the fall, so the God-restored man, Jesus, recovered what was stolen. Both had divinely engineered DNA.

1 John 3:8   He who sins is of the devil, for the devil has sinned from the beginning. <u>For this purpose the Son of God was manifested, that He might destroy the works of the devil</u>.

Adam was a son of God, just like Jesus, but it appears that he was formed and not made by direct intervention.

Genesis 2:7   And the LORD God formed man of the dust of the ground, and breathed into his nostrils the breath of life; and man became a living being.

YHVH wasn't with Jesus on the cross. It was Jesus, the man, who bore our sins alone. God and sin

What If Scriptures—Vol. 1

are like matter and antimatter. They cannot exist in the same place. Neither can God be cursed.

Deuteronomy 21:22-23   If a man has committed a sin deserving of death, and he is put to death, and you hang him on a tree, ²³his body shall not remain overnight on the tree, but you shall surely bury him that day, so that you do not defile the land which the LORD your God is giving you as an inheritance; for he who is hanged is accursed of God.

God cannot curse Himself.

Matthew 27:46   And about the ninth hour Jesus cried out with a loud voice, saying, "Eli, Eli, lama sabachthani?" that is, "My God, My God, why have You forsaken Me?"

Or "Why have You left me?"

1 Timothy 2:5-6   For *there is* one God and one Mediator between God and men, *the* Man Christ Jesus, ⁶who gave Himself a ransom for all, to be testified in due time … .

It was because Jesus fulfilled the role and prophecies of the Messiah that He became the Christ.

So now it appears that we have these four:

1. Most High God Y-H

What If Scriptures—Vol. 1

2. God of the Elohiym, Abraham, Isaac, and Jacob (YHVH)
3. Spirit of the Elohiym (Holy Spirit)
4. The only begotten Son of God (Jesus) who became the Christ

The first three form the Trinity.

Now Philippians make sense, but you will need to think about it.

Philippians 2:5-11 Let this mind be in you which was also in Christ Jesus, [6] who, being in the form of God, did not consider it robbery to be equal with God, [7] but made Himself of no reputation, taking the form of a bondservant, *and* coming in the likeness of men. [8] And being found in appearance as a man, He humbled Himself and became obedient to *the point of* death, even the death of the cross. [9] Therefore God also has highly exalted Him and given Him the name which is above every name, [10] that at the name of Jesus every knee should bow, of those in heaven, and of those on earth, and of those under the earth, [11] and *that* every tongue should confess that Jesus Christ *is* Lord, to the glory of God the Father.

In essence, Jesus has retaken what Satan took from Adam and YHVH has put Him in charge of this

What If Scriptures—Vol. 1

Heaven and earth. And He is coming back to reign until a new heaven and earth are ready.

Restoration comes through Jesus Christ, but transformation comes through the Holy Spirit.

Romans 8:29-30   For whom He foreknew, He also predestined *to be* conformed to the image of His Son, that He might be the firstborn among many brethren. ³⁰ Moreover whom He predestined, these He also called; whom He called, these He also justified; and whom He justified, these He also glorified.

Sometimes it's confusing who all the pronouns and are referring to, so I took the liberty of inserting to whom I thought they were referring.

What if the above scripture read: "For whom He [Y-H] foreknew, He [Y-H] also predestined *to be* conformed to the image of His Son [YHVH], that He [Jesus] might be the firstborn among many brethren. Moreover, whom He [Y-H] predestined, these He [Y-H] also called; whom He [Y-H] called, these He [Y-H] also justified; and whom He [Y-H] justified, these He [Y-H] also glorified.

What If Scriptures—Vol. 1

Doesn't this indicate that Jesus was conformed to the Son's image, implying that he wasn't God to begin with?

Genesis 1:26   Then God [Elohiym] said, "Let Us make man in Our image, according to Our likeness; let them have dominion over the fish of the sea, over the birds of the air, and over the cattle, over all the earth and over every creeping thing that creeps on the earth."

Don't Adam and Jesus fulfill everything in the above verse?

Aren't we to be like Jesus, but in the image of YHVH?

1 John 3:2   Beloved, now we are children of God; and it has not yet been revealed what we shall be, but we know <u>that when He is revealed, we shall be like Him, for we shall see Him as He is</u>.

Who is the "He" and "Him" in the above verse? You think it's Jesus?

We will be transformed into a new body with the same DNA as Jesus. One that does not have a sin nature. The difference from the original Adam is that now we know the difference between good and evil and have chosen God, Love, of our own free will.

What If Scriptures—Vol. 1

This step is not the end of the line, but the first in a process until we look like Him (YHVH).

Will the new bodies be male and female? I don't know, but:

Galatians 3:28   There is neither Jew nor Greek, there is neither slave nor free, <u>there is neither male nor female</u>; for you are all one in Christ Jesus.

What about John 1?

John 1:1-14   In the beginning was the Word, and the Word was with God, and the Word was God. ² He was in the beginning with God. ³ All things were made through Him, and without Him nothing was made that was made. ⁴ In Him was life, and the life was the light of men. ⁵ And the light shines in the darkness, and the darkness did not comprehend it.

⁶ There was a man sent from God, whose name *was* John. ⁷ This man came for a witness, to bear witness of the Light, that all through him might believe. ⁸ He was not that Light, but *was sent* to bear witness of that Light. ⁹ That was the true Light which gives light to every man coming into the world.

What If Scriptures—Vol. 1

¹⁰ He was in the world, and the world was made through Him, and the world did not know Him. ¹¹ He came to His own, and His own did not receive Him. ¹² But as many as received Him, to them He gave the right to become children of God, to those who believe in His name: ¹³ who were born, not of blood, nor of the will of the flesh, nor of the will of man, but of God.

¹⁴ And the Word became flesh and dwelt among us, and we beheld His glory, the glory as of the only begotten of the Father, full of grace and truth.

The word *Word* (Greek *logos*) in this scripture can also mean "thought or reason."

What if it read: "In the beginning was the thought of Jesus and this thought was with God and met His purpose. God had this thought from the beginning and everything that was made was made to fulfill this thought. In this thought would be the life and light of mankind and the enemies of God would not comprehend it ... .

"And this thought became real through Jesus Christ and dwelt among us, showing us the glory of His Father and revealing the Father's grace and truth to us."

What If Scriptures—Vol. 1

Revelation 13:8   All who dwell on the earth will worship him, whose names have not been written in the Book of Life of the Lamb slain from the foundation of the world.

Similarly, in the above verse Jesus wasn't literally slain before the foundation of the world, but it was the thought of God that He would be. Also, who is the "Him" who will be worshiped here? If it is the Lamb, wouldn't it be worded differently to remove any ambiguity?

Isaiah 9:6   For unto us a child is born, unto us a son is given: and the government shall be upon his shoulder: and his name shall be called Wonderful, Counselor, The mighty God, The everlasting Father, The Prince of Peace.

Why are "child" and "son" in separate clauses unless it's referring to the child Jesus and the son YHVH?

What if I read this, 'For unto us a child [Jesus] is born, unto us a son [YHVH] is given'?

Jesus is not referred to as the mighty God and everlasting Father; YHVH is.

What If Scriptures—Vol. 1

John 8:58   Jesus said to them, "Most assuredly, I say to you, before Abraham was, I AM."

If Jesus said what the Father was saying, then wasn't it the Father saying this through Jesus?

John 17:21   that they all may be one, as You, Father, *are* in Me, and I in You; that they also may be one in Us, that the world may believe that You sent Me.

Jesus isn't saying He and the Father are the same person. If I am to be just like Jesus, with my relationship to the Father in me by His Spirit, am I then God?. Heaven forbid! What Jesus is saying is that the Father is dwelling in Him by virtue of His Spirit and that they are in unity.

John 14:23   Jesus answered and said to him, "If anyone loves Me, he will keep My word; and My Father will love him, and We will come to him and make Our home with him. [24] He who does not love Me does not keep My words; and the word which you hear is not Mine but the Father's who sent Me.

Here Jesus is saying the same thing, that He and the Father will take up residence in those who show their love for them by keeping their commandments.

What If Scriptures—Vol. 1

I think that when Jesus said, "I say to you," "Verily, verily," or other such prefaces, what follows are the Father's words. What do you think?

One more thing. Jesus' name in Hebrew is Yeshua. If He was given a new name, referring to the Philippians verse, is there a precedent to what it might be?

Genesis 17:3-5   Then Abram fell on his face, and God talked with him, saying: [4]"As for Me, behold, My covenant is with you, and you shall be a father of many nations. [5]No longer shall your name be called Abram, but your name shall be Abraham; for I have made you a father of many nations.

Genesis 17:15   Then God said to Abraham, "As for Sarai your wife, you shall not call her name Sarai, but Sarah *shall be* her name."

It appears in both cases of new names YHVH added or replaced a vowel with 'ah'. If I do the same with Yeshua, I can get Yahshua, which means Y-H saves. I think I see a pattern here. It could also reinforce that Y-H is not an abbreviation of YHVH.

One of the arguments that Jesus is God is that only God can forgive sins and because Jesus did,

What If Scriptures—Vol. 1

therefore He is God. If that is true, then what about the following scripture.

John 20:21-23   So Jesus said to them again, "Peace to you! As the Father has sent Me, I also send you." <u>²²And when He had said this, He breathed on *them,* and said to them, "Receive the Holy Spirit. ²³If you forgive the sins of any, they are forgiven them; if you retain the *sins* of any, they are retained</u>."

One more scripture.

Revelation 1:6   "And hath made us kings and priests unto God and his Father; to him *be* glory and dominion forever and ever. Amen." (KJV)

Revelation 1:6   And he has made us The Priestly Kingdom to God and his Father; to him be glory and Empire to the eternity of eternities. Amen. (The Aramaic Bible)

While most people and some translations read this as "priests unto his God and Father," could it be "priests unto God [YHVH] and His Father [Y-H]"? The problem is the "and." Either way you read it, it appears that Jesus is not God.

What If Scriptures—Vol. 1

Remember, Jesus is the way, but the Father is the destination.

Some say, "All you need is Jesus, all you need is the Father, or all you need is the Holy Spirit," but I believe I need them all.

I am not saying this is ultimate truth. I am saying that this is what has been given to me. I didn't read or hear it anywhere else. There is a lot more, but I don't feel led to give every scripture or over-explain.

Has this "What If" changed your perspective or caused you to get more revelation?

All I ask is that you pray about it before screaming "Blasphemy"!

CHAPTER 2

Puzzling Scripture #2

Genesis 1:1 In the beginning God created the heavens and the earth.

The Hebrew word for *God* here is *Elohiym*. Elohiym is the plural form of El (God). The standard Christian theological reason for this is that it is referring to the Trinity.

What if it isn't.

I have yet to read any coherent reason why the word *Elohiym* was used instead of El or Eloah. There are other scriptures where the word *Elohiym* is used which appear to be singular. Is the word *American* singular or plural? *American* could refer to a group of people or a single person. In this first verse, there is nothing to help us delineate the intended sense. In this case, we must trust it as written—plural.

Other Hebrew words ending with the sound "eem".

Nephilim – The supposed offspring of fallen angels in Genesis 6

Anakim – giants

What If Scriptures—Vol. 1

The ending "ites" most often refers to descendants of a person, including a regional reference, whereas "im" usually refers to a race of people.

The way I read Genesis 1:1 is:

In the beginning *the* Elohiym created the heavens and the earth.

All references to God in Genesis 1 are the word *Elohiym*.

If the heavens and the earth were created in verse 1, why is it assumed that the rest of the chapter is an explanation of it?

See my other books for discussions of this and what was in the Forward about it being an allegory.

In Genesis 2 we are introduced to "Lord God" or YHVH Elohiym. The way it's translated both YHVH and Elohiym are titles, Lord God, with YHVH also being a proper name.

What if YHVH Elohiym means YHVH, proper name, of the Elohiym or as a title God of Lords?

So, while all the heavens and the earth were created by the Elohiym, our heaven and earth come under the jurisdiction of a specific person, YHVH. Or it

What If Scriptures—Vol. 1

could be that YHVH is the senior or head of the Elohiym.

As one of the Elohiym, nothing that was made was made without Him, YHVH.

John 1:3   All things were made through Him, and without Him nothing was made that was made.

You think that this refers to Jesus? There are many other scriptures that say YHVH created the heavens and earth.

I am building off the conclusions of the first chapter and previous books, especially *The Ultimate Simulation*.

What does Psalm 82 really say?

Psalm 82   God stands in the congregation of the mighty; He judges among the gods.
² How long will you judge unjustly, and show partiality to the wicked? *Selah*
³ Defend the poor and fatherless; do justice to the afflicted and needy.
⁴ Deliver the poor and needy; free *them* from the hand of the wicked.

⁵ They do not know, nor do they understand; they walk about in darkness;
All the foundations of the earth are unstable.

⁶ I said, "You *are* gods, and all of you *are* children of the Most High.
⁷ But you shall die like men, and fall like one of the princes."

⁸ Arise, O God, judge the earth; for You shall inherit all nations.

Let me put in the Hebrew words for *God*, *gods*, and *mighty*.

God [Elohiym, referring to YHVH] stands in the congregation of the mighty [El, most high God]; [Y-H]? He [YHVH] judges among the gods [Elohiym].
² How long will you judge unjustly, and show partiality to the wicked? *Selah*
³ Defend the poor and fatherless; do justice to the afflicted and needy.
⁴ Deliver the poor and needy; free *them* from the hand of the wicked.

What If Scriptures—Vol. 1

⁵ They do not know, nor do they understand; they walk about in darkness;
All the foundations of the earth are unstable.

⁶ I said [Y-H], "You *are* gods [Elohiym], and all of you *are* children of the Most High [Elyon, Y-H].
⁷ But you shall die like men, and fall like one of the princes [Satan]."

⁸ Arise, O God [Elohiym, YHVH], judge the earth; for You [YHVH] shall inherit all nations.

Who's talking here, if not Y-H?

Therefore, according to Psalm 82, the Elohiym are children of the Most High God and, it appears, YHVH judges among them. Since YHVH is one of the Elohiym, then He is a Son of the Most High, Y-H.

Then there is the first commandment.

Exodus 20:3   You shall have no other gods [Elohiym] before Me.

Concerning the Holy Spirit.

Genesis 1:2   The earth was without form, and void; and darkness *was* on the face of the deep. And the <u>Spirit of God</u> was hovering over the face of the waters.

What If Scriptures—Vol. 1

The Spirit of God is the Spirit of the Elohiym.

The Holy Trinity is therefore: God the Father (Y-H), God the Son (YHVH) and the Holy Spirit (of the Elohiym).

Psalm 102:18 This will be written for the generation to come, that a people yet to be created may praise Y-H.

It appears that in the last days, people will praise Y-H.

What is the Holy Spirit saying to you about what you just read?

CHAPTER 3

Puzzling Scripture #3

Isaiah 43:10   "You are My witnesses," says the LORD [YHVH], "And My servant whom I have chosen, that you may know and believe Me, and understand that I am He. <u>Before Me there was no God formed, nor shall there be after Me</u>."

This is YHVH talking. The word here for *God* is *Elohiym.* So, what He is saying isn't that there was no God formed before Him, but rather there was no Elohiym formed before Him. This implies He is the first son of Y-H.

So much for the eternal nature of the Elohiym and thereby YHVH. Unless the Elohiym were a created race by Y-H and it is He (Y-H) that is eternal.

YHVH can't be the only Elohiym because of Psalm 82. See Chapter 2.

Also,

Psalm 95:3   For the LORD *is* the great God, And the great King above all gods.

What If Scriptures—Vol. 1

The above verse reads, "For YHVH is the great El and the great King above all Elohiym."

This seems to negate my assertions about Y-H. When you read the surrounding verses, they only point to YHVH as the top Elohiym.

Psalm 95:1-7 Oh come, let us sing to the LORD [YHVH]! Let us shout joyfully to the <u>Rock of our salvation</u>.
² Let us come before His presence with thanksgiving; Let us shout joyfully to Him with psalms.
³ For the LORD [YHVH] *is* the great God [El], and the great King above all gods [Elohiym].
⁴ In His hand *are* the deep places of the earth; the heights of the hills *are* His also.
⁵ The sea *is* His, for He made it; and His hands formed the dry *land.*
⁶ Oh come, let us worship and bow down; let us kneel before the LORD [YHVH] our Maker.
⁷ <u>For He *is* our God [Elohiym], and we *are* the people of His pasture, and the sheep of His hand.</u>

Who is the Rock of our salvation? It could be Jesus, but all these verses are about YHVH.

What do you think?

CHAPTER 4

Puzzling Scripture #4

Psalm 8   O L ORD, our Lord,
How excellent *is* Your name in all the earth,
Who have set Your glory above the heavens!

² Out of the mouth of babes and nursing infants
You have ordained strength,

Because of Your enemies,

That You may silence the enemy and the avenger.

³ When I consider Your heavens, the work of Your fingers,
The moon and the stars, which You have ordained,

⁴ What is man that You are mindful of him,
And the son of man that You visit him?

⁵For You have made him a little lower than the angels,
And You have crowned him with glory and honor.

⁶ You have made him to have dominion over the works of Your hands;

You have put all *things* under his feet,

⁷ All sheep and oxen—
Even the beasts of the field,

⁸ The birds of the air,

What If Scriptures—Vol. 1

And the fish of the sea
That pass through the paths of the seas.

⁹ O LORD, our Lord,
How excellent *is* Your name in all the earth!

In verses 1 and 9, it reads "O YHVH, our Lord." By this, we know who this psalm is about.

In verse 5, I believe this is the only place in the Bible where the word *Elohiym* is translated as angels.

It literally reads: "For You have made him a little lower than the Elohiym."

Does this refer to Adam, Jesus, mankind, or all three?

Does Jesus, the YHVH-engineered man, have dominion over angels? No.

Matthew 26:53   Or do you think that I cannot now pray to My Father, and He will provide Me with more than twelve legions of angels?

If He would need to ask His Father, then He doesn't have dominion.

Paul quoted Psalm 8 in Hebrews.

What If Scriptures—Vol. 1

Hebrews 2:6-9 But one testified in a certain place, saying:

"What is man that You are mindful of him,
Or the son of man that You take care of him?
⁷ You have made him a little lower than the angels;
You have crowned him with glory and honor,
And set him over the works of Your hands.
⁸ You have put all things in subjection under his feet."

For in that He put all in subjection under him, He left nothing *that is* not put under him. But now we do not yet see all things put under him. ⁹ <u>But we see Jesus, who was made a little lower than the angels</u>, for the suffering of death crowned with glory and honor, that He, by the grace of God, might taste death for everyone.

Paul clearly defines Jesus as being made lower than angels. Most people argue that this is the position He took.

What do you think?

In the New American Standard Version of the Bible, both Psalm 8:5 and Hebrews 2:7 read:

What If Scriptures—Vol. 1

You have made him a little lower than God,

Bible versions are split fairly evenly on the translation of *Elohiym* in these two verses.

There is a second puzzle in Psalm 8. Verse 2 doesn't seem to belong.

[2] Out of the mouth of babes and nursing infants
You have ordained strength,
Because of Your enemies,
That You may silence the enemy and the avenger.

I thought about this for quite a while. Then, while talking to a friend about it, I got this:

What if the babes and nursing infants in verse 2 refer to man and the son of man in verse 6. In other words, YHVH has destined this imperfect creation to be victorious over His enemies. The difference between man and son of man being that the son of man is nursing at the breast of El Shaddai, the many-breasted God.

1 Peter 1:10-12   Of this salvation the prophets have inquired and searched carefully, who prophesied of the grace *that would come* to you, [11] searching what, or what

What If Scriptures—Vol. 1

manner of time, the Spirit of Christ who was in them was indicating when He testified beforehand the sufferings of Christ and the glories that would follow. [12] To them it was revealed that, not to themselves, but to us they were ministering the things which now have been reported to you through those who have preached the gospel to you by the Holy Spirit sent from heaven—<u>things which angels desire to look into.</u>

Why did Jesus come?

1 John 3:8   He who sins is of the devil, for the devil has sinned from the beginning. <u>For this purpose the Son of God was manifested, that He might destroy the works of the devil</u>.

Romans 8:28-32   And we know that all things work together for good to those who love God, to those who are the called according to *His* purpose. [29] For whom He foreknew, He also predestined *to be* conformed to the image of His Son, that He might be the firstborn among many brethren. [30] Moreover whom He predestined, these He also called; whom He called, these He also justified; and whom He justified, these He also glorified.

[31] What then shall we say to these things? If God *is* for us, who *can be* against us? [32] He who did not spare His own

What If Scriptures—Vol. 1

Son, but delivered Him up for us all, how shall He not with Him also freely give us all things?

There are a lot of pronouns in the above verse, and not all of them refer to the same person. I always read this as follows:

²⁸ And we [saints] know that all things work together for good to those who love God, to those who are the called [those who respond to the call] according to *His* [God's] purpose. ²⁹ For whom He [God] foreknew, He [God] also predestined *to be* conformed to the image of His [God's] Son [YHVH], that He [Jesus] might be the firstborn among many brethren. ³⁰ Moreover whom He [God] predestined, these He [God] also called; whom He [God] called, these He [God] also justified; and whom He [God] justified, these He [God] also glorified.

³¹ What then shall we say to these things? If God *is* for us, who *can be* against us? ³² He [God] who did not spare His own Son [Jesus], but delivered Him [Jesus] up for us all, how shall He [God] not with Him [Jesus] also freely give us all things?

Then there is this:

What If Scriptures—Vol. 1

Genesis 1:26   Then God said, "Let Us make man in Our image, according to Our likeness; let them have dominion over the fish of the sea, over the birds of the air, and over the cattle, over all the earth and over every creeping thing that creeps on the earth."

The word *God* in the above verse is *Elohiym*. So, whose image are we made in—Jesus', Elohiym's or both?

In Romans 8:32 "His own Son" clearly points to Jesus, and because of this we assume the same for verse 29.

What if it isn't.

What if verses 29 and 30 read as follows:

Romans 8:29-30   For whom He [Y-H] foreknew, He [Y-H] also predestined *to be* conformed to the image of His [Y-H's] Son [YHVH], that He [Jesus] might be the firstborn among many brethren. ³⁰ Moreover whom He [Y-H] predestined, these He [Y-H] also called; whom He [Y-H] called, these He [Y-H] also justified; and whom He [Y-H] justified, these He [Y-H] also glorified.

What If Scriptures—Vol. 1

This would appear to bring it in line with Genesis 1:26.

What do you think?

CHAPTER 5

Puzzling Scripture #5

Hebrews 9:27   And as it is appointed for men to die once, but after this the judgment.

Matthew 17:1-3   Now after six days Jesus took Peter, James, and John his brother, led them up on a high mountain by themselves; ² and He was transfigured before them. His face shone like the sun, and His clothes became as white as the light. ³ And behold, <u>Moses and Elijah appeared to them, talking with Him</u>.

If Moses and Elijah were dead, was Jesus committing necromancy by talking to them?

You might say that Elijah didn't die, but Moses did.

Moses and Elijah have something in common. They were both in a cave or cleft on Mt Sinai.

What if YHVH brought them forward in time to talk to Jesus at a time when they both needed encouragement by showing them the One who was promised? Is there a time portal on Mt. Sinai?

What If Scriptures—Vol. 1

While we're on the subject:

Malachi 4:5   Behold, I will send you Elijah the prophet before the coming of the great and dreadful day of the LORD.

For those who don't know, the great day of the Lord was Jesus' first coming. The terrible day of the Lord will be His second.

Matthew 11:12-14   And from the days of John the Baptist until now the kingdom of heaven suffers violence, and the violent take it by force. [13] For all the prophets and the law prophesied until John. [14] And if you are willing to receive *it,* he is Elijah who is to come.

There are many theories about this. Some say that John the Baptist had the spirit of Elijah. Even though John said he wasn't Elijah doesn't mean that he wasn't. It means that if he was, he didn't know it. I believe if Jesus said it, he was.

Now to the main question: Even though Elijah didn't die, but was carried up to Heaven in a whirlwind, John the Baptist did die. If Elijah is to come again before the terrible day of the Lord, how do I get around the once-to-die scripture?

What If Scriptures—Vol. 1

The only feasible answer is that John was judged. There is nothing in scripture about coming back after judgment. Or that he would appear on earth like an angel, not that he became an angel.

It appears that Jesus was already judged when he died, because He got a new name and is seated at the right hand of YHVH.

I still don't know.

Didn't the Shunammite's son, Lazarus, and Jairus's daughter all die twice? How do you reconcile this scripture about once to die for those raised from the dead? If you say they were judged after the first death, then were there no consequences or judgment upon their second death? Or were they judged twice. Either way, I don't understand it.

Some argue that these weren't resurrected but revived. I guess this is like "Princess Bride," where they were "mostly dead." (Forgive the sarcasm).

John 11:14   Then said Jesus unto them plainly, Lazarus is dead.

What If Scriptures—Vol. 1

One more question: If we are in the last days and the terrible day of the Lord is approaching, where is Elijah? Who today is preaching repentance and remission of sin?

Luke 24:46-47   Then He said to them, "Thus it is written, and thus it was necessary for the Christ to suffer and to rise from the dead the third day, [47] and that repentance and remission of sins should be preached in His name to all nations, beginning at Jerusalem.

What do you think?

CHAPTER 6

Puzzling Scripture #6

Genesis 11:1-7   Now the whole earth had one language and one speech. ² And it came to pass, as they journeyed from the east, that they found a plain in the land of Shinar, and they dwelt there. ³ Then they said to one another, "Come, let us make bricks and bake *them* thoroughly." They had brick for stone, and they had asphalt for mortar. ⁴ And they said, "Come, let us build ourselves a city, and a tower whose top *is* in the heavens; let us make a name for ourselves, lest we be scattered abroad over the face of the whole earth."

⁵ But the LORD came down to see the city and the tower which the sons of men had built. ⁶ And the LORD said, "Indeed the people *are* one and they all have one language, and this is what they begin to do; now nothing that they propose to do will be withheld from them. ⁷ Come, let Us go down and there confuse their language, that they may not understand one another's speech."

Why did YHVH have to come down to see what man was doing, and why did YHVH say, "Come, let Us go down," if He and the Elohiym are omnipresent?

What If Scriptures—Vol. 1

Again:

Genesis 18:20   And the LORD said, "Because the outcry against Sodom and Gomorrah is great, and because their sin is very grave, <u>²¹ I will go down now and see whether they have done altogether according to the outcry against it that has come to Me; and if not, I will know</u>."

Why does the Lord need to go and see if He is omnipresent?

Perhaps, it is only Y-H and the Holy Spirit who are omnipresent and YHVH and the Elohiym are not. If YHVH is not omnipresent than neither Jesus nor any other son of the Elohiym are either, including Satan.

Psalm 139:7-8   Where shall I go from Your Spirit? Or where can I flee from Your presence? ⁸ If I ascend into heaven, You *are* there; If I make my bed in hell, behold, You *are there*.

Hebrew gives this a different perspective.

Psalm 139:7-8   Where can I go from Your Spirit? Or where from Your face shall I flee? ⁸ If I go up to heaven, there You (*are*); If I make my bed in Sheol, You behold (*are there*). (Interlinear Bible)

What If Scriptures—Vol. 1

I think verse 8 is referring to His face from verse 7. If so, then potentially what this is saying is that the Holy Spirit is omnipresent, but whether I go to Heaven or Sheol, Your face is always before me. This is different than saying YHVH is omnipresent.

Note: Whenever words in the Bible are in *italics*, it means they were added by the translator for clarification for what the translator thought it meant, but they aren't there in the original.

As a side note, I believe Genesis 11:6 is one of the most interesting verses in the Bible.

Genesis 11:6 And the LORD said, "Indeed the people *are* one and they all have one language, and this is what they begin to do; <u>now nothing that they propose to do will be withheld from them</u>."

This verse shows the power of belief coupled with unity, not the power of faith. It appears that there are no boundaries, except ones that God has the angels enforce. I know boundaries exist because a long time ago I hit one. I will not talk about it here, nor will I ever go close to it again.

What do you think?

What If Scriptures—Vol. 1

CHAPTER 7

Where Is the Throne of God?

This chapter isn't about a specific scripture, but rather a concept expressed in different scriptures. The question is "Where is the throne of God?"

Throne: In Hebrew, the word *kis-say* comes from *kaw-saw,* which means "to cover, conceal or hide." It implies a royal dignitary, authority, and power.

In the Greek, the word *thronos* comes from *thrao*, which means "to sit." Sitting is a metaphor for authority and power. When the king sat on his throne, everyone else stood.

Psalm 11:4   The LORD *is* in His holy temple, The LORD's throne *is* in heaven.

Matthew 5:34   But I say to you, do not swear at all: neither by heaven, for it is God's throne.

Acts 7:49   "Heaven *is* My throne, and earth *is* My footstool.
What house will you build for Me?" says the LORD, "Or what *is* the place of My rest?"

What If Scriptures—Vol. 1

It only makes sense that His throne is at the pinnacle of the heavens, out of which flows all authority and power.

But wait, there is another scripture.

Revelation 22 1:1-5   And he showed me a pure river of water of life, clear as crystal, <u>proceeding from the throne of God and of the Lamb</u>. ² In the middle of its street, and on either side of the river, *was* the tree of life, which bore twelve fruits, each *tree* yielding its fruit every month. The leaves of the tree *were* for the healing of the nations. ³ And there shall be no more curse, but the throne of God and of the Lamb shall be in it, and His servants shall serve Him. ⁴ They shall see His face, and His name *shall be* on their foreheads. ⁵ There shall be no night there: They need no lamp nor light of the sun, for the Lord God gives them light. And they shall reign forever and ever.

This throne is in New Jerusalem. Does YHVH leave His throne in the third heaven for another in New Jerusalem? It appears so. In that case, who is on the throne in the third heaven? You may say He is omnipresent, but we have already covered scriptures that indicate He isn't. Or is He there by virtue of His Spirit? Or does another Elohiym take control while YHVH finishes His work of making Sons?

What If Scriptures—Vol. 1

But wait, there is another possibility.

A king's throne is always in his kingdom.

Luke 17:20-21   Now when He was asked by the Pharisees when the kingdom of God would come, He answered them and said, "The kingdom of God does not come with observation; [21] nor will they say, 'See here!' or 'See there!' <u>For indeed, the kingdom of God is within you</u>."

If the Kingdom of Heaven is within you, so shouldn't His throne be there too? Or is this a metaphor for the only way the Kingdom can operate through you is for there to be absolute obedience to the King as if His throne were there?

John 14:23   Jesus answered and said to him, "If anyone loves Me, he will keep My word; and My Father will love him, and <u>We will come to him and make Our home with him</u>."

Is this strictly by the Holy Spirit or all of the above?

The throne in Heaven is always the throne of YHVH. Jesus is seated at the right hand of YHVH. Whose will be the future throne on the earth?

What If Scriptures—Vol. 1

I guess this isn't about where *His throne* is, as much as where *He* is.

Who do you think is going to judge the earth, Jesus, YHVH, or possibly the Ancient of Days? There appear to be scriptures that point to all three.

What do you think?

CHAPTER 8

Who Was Melchizedek?

Genesis 14:18-20   Then Melchizedek king of Salem brought out bread and wine; he *was* the priest of God Most High. [19] And he blessed him and said: "Blessed be Abram of God Most High, Possessor of heaven and earth; [20] and blessed be God Most High, Who has delivered your enemies into your hand." And he gave him a tithe of all.

This priest/king of Salem came out of nowhere and was recognized as a priest of the Most High God. (Salem was the forerunner of Jerusalem.)

There are several different translations of the name.
    1. King of Righteousness
    2. My King is Righteousness
I prefer the later.

The only other place in the Old Testament he is mentioned is Psalm 110.

Psalm 110:1-4   "Sit at My right hand, Till I make Your enemies Your footstool."
[2] The LORD shall send the rod of Your strength out of Zion.

What If Scriptures—Vol. 1

Rule in the midst of Your enemies! ³ Your people *shall be* volunteers in the day of Your power;
In the beauties of holiness, from the womb of the morning, You have the dew of Your youth.
⁴ The LORD has sworn and will not relent,
"You *are* a priest forever according to the order of Melchizedek."

In the above scripture, Lord is YHVH. Who is seated at the right hand of YHVH? It is talking about the millennial reign of Jesus and declares Him to be "a priest forever after the order of Melchizedek."

The only other place Melchizedek is mentioned is in Hebrews 5-7. There Paul was explaining how Jesus can be High Priest when He was not in the lineage of Aaron or even of the Levites, as dictated by the Law for normal priests.

In Hebrews 7, Paul tells us all we know about where he came from.

Hebrews 7:1-3   For this Melchizedek, king of Salem, priest of the Most High God, who met Abraham returning from the slaughter of the kings and blessed him, ² to whom also Abraham gave a tenth part of all, first being translated "king of righteousness," and then also king of Salem, meaning "king of peace," [3] without father, without mother, without genealogy, having neither beginning of days nor end of life, but made like the Son of God, remains a priest continually.

He is definitely a type of Christ, but is he Jesus? It says he wasn't born, nor did he die, but rather appears to play a role necessary to complete YHVH's purpose and plan.

First, because there was an "order" which Melchizedek belonged to, then he cannot be the only one. Jesus is now a member of this order.

What I'm being told is that Melchizedek is a member of a group of heavenly beings that are priests unto YHVH. In addition to serving Him, YHVH sends them on special missions to fulfill tasks no human is able or available to accomplish in the furtherance of His will.

How can Jesus be a member of this order? One of the main roles of a priest is to intercede before God on behalf of others. Further, in Hebrews, Paul explains that Jesus' work continues on our behalf.

What If Scriptures—Vol. 1

Hebrews 7:25   Therefore He is also able to save to the uttermost those who come to God through Him, <u>since He always lives to make intercession for them</u>.

If we who believe are saved, why does He need to intercede?

Exodus 19:6   "'And unto Me you shall be a kingdom of priests and a holy nation.' These are the words that you are to speak to the Israelites."

Revelation 1:6   And he has made us The Priestly Kingdom to God and his Father; to him be glory and Empire to the eternity of eternities. Amen. (The Aramaic Bible)

What if we are predestined to become priests to our God, after the order of Melchizedek as part of the process? Isn't intercession an act of love?

What do you think?

CHAPTER 9

Puzzling Scripture #7

John 3:13-17   No one has ascended to heaven but He who came down from heaven, *that is,* the Son of Man who is in heaven. ¹⁴ And as Moses lifted up the serpent in the wilderness, even so must the Son of Man be lifted up,

¹⁵ that whoever believes in Him should not perish but have eternal life. ¹⁶ For God so loved the world that He gave His only begotten Son, that whoever believes in Him should not perish but have everlasting life. ¹⁷ For God did not send His Son into the world to condemn the world, but that the world through Him might be saved.

Why doesn't it say, "For God so loved people"?

Why in verses 13 and 14 does it say, "Son of Man," and in verses 16 and 17 it uses "His Son"?

1 John 4:8   He who does not love does not know God, for God is love.

One of the problems I have with this verse is that most people believe that love is all that He is, and therefore, they conclude that He loves everybody.

What If Scriptures—Vol. 1

Psalm 5:4-6 For You *are* not a God who takes pleasure in wickedness, nor shall evil dwell with You.
⁵ The boastful shall not stand in Your sight; <u>You hate all workers of iniquity</u>.
⁶ <u>You shall destroy those who speak falsehood; the LORD [YHVH] abhors the bloodthirsty and deceitful man</u>.

Psalm 97:10 <u>You who love the LORD [YHVH], hate evil</u>! He preserves the souls of His saints; He delivers them out of the hand of the wicked.

Proverbs 6:16-19 <u>These six *things* the LORD [YHVH] hates, yes, seven *are* an abomination to Him</u>:
¹⁷ A proud look, a lying tongue, hands that shed innocent blood,
¹⁸ A heart that devises wicked plans, feet that are swift in running to evil,
¹⁹ A false witness *who* speaks lies, and one who sows discord among brethren.

Proverbs 8:17 <u>I love those who love me</u>, and those who seek me diligently will find me.

You may say, "That's Old Testament. Jesus isn't like that." But in the Parable of the Talents, see what Jesus said.

What If Scriptures—Vol. 1

Luke 19:26-27   <u>He replied, "I tell you that to everyone who has, more will be given, but as for the one who has nothing, even what they have will be taken away. ²⁷ But those enemies of mine who did not want me to be king over them—bring them here and kill them in front of me."</u>

Did Jesus not love them?

Romans 6:23   For the wages of sin *is* death, but the gift of God *is* eternal life in Christ Jesus our Lord.

Genesis 6:5-12   Then the LORD saw that the wickedness of man *was* great in the earth, and *that* every intent of the thoughts of his heart *was* only evil continually. ⁶ And the LORD was sorry that He had made man on the earth, and He was grieved in His heart. ⁷ So the LORD said, "I will destroy man whom I have created from the face of the earth, both man and beast, creeping thing and birds of the air, for I am sorry that I have made them." ⁸ But Noah found grace in the eyes of the LORD.

Did YHVH destroy the people with a flood because He loved them?

How about the people of Sodom and Gomorrah?

What If Scriptures—Vol. 1

Revelation 3:14-16   And to the angel of the church of the Laodiceans write, "These things says the Amen, the Faithful and True Witness, the Beginning of the creation of God: [15] 'I know your works, that you are neither cold nor hot. I could wish you were cold or hot. [16] <u>So then, because you are lukewarm, and neither cold nor hot, I will vomit you out of My mouth.</u>'"

    Jesus is not a nice man. He called the Pharisees "snakes" and "tombs full of dead men's bones." He called a Samaritan woman a dog. He said of people that harm children, "It would be better for him if a millstone were hung around his neck, and he were thrown into the sea, than that he should offend one of these little ones."

    But He is just, truthful, and full of mercy and grace for those who diligently seek and love Him.

    I can only come to one conclusion: God and Jesus do not love everyone.

    God loves those who strive to conform to His will. Grace and mercy are only available to those who still have potential to become sons (His will). The only way to lose with Him is to quit.

What If Scriptures—Vol. 1

Let me give you Tom's version of John 3:13-17:

John 3:13-17   No one has ascended to heaven but He who came down from heaven, *that is,* the Son of Man [Jesus] who is in heaven. [14] And as Moses lifted up the serpent in the wilderness, even so must the Son of Man [Jesus] be lifted up, [15] that whoever believes in Him should not perish but have eternal life. [16] For God [Y-H] so loved the world [that has the potential to produce sons, thereby fulfilling His will] that He gave His only begotten Son [YHVH and/or Jesus], that whoever believes in Him should not perish but have everlasting life. [17] For God did not send His Son [YHVH and/or Jesus] into the world to condemn the world, but that the world through Him might be saved.

If YHVH is the only begotten Son of Y-H and Jesus is the only begotten son of YHVH, then who is the Son referred to in verses 16 and 17. Since verses 13 and 14 delineate Jesus as the Son of Man, it would appear to point to YHVH. Regardless, Y-H is an awesome God, YHVH is an awesome Lord, and Jesus is an awesome King.

What do you think?

CHAPTER 10

Psalms of Blessing

In this chapter, I want to present psalms of blessing and psalms that are for the millennial reign. I've added the Hebrew word for Lord and also for Jesus for clarification, highlighting the previous conclusions.

Psalm 112   <u>Praise the LORD [Y-H]! Blessed *is* the man *who* fears the LORD [YHVH], *who* delights greatly in His commandments.</u>

² His descendants will be mighty on earth; the generation of the upright will be blessed.

³ Wealth and riches *will be* in his house, and his righteousness endures forever.

⁴ Unto the upright there arises light in the darkness; *he is* gracious, and full of compassion, and righteous.

⁵ A good man deals graciously and lends; he will guide his affairs with discretion.

⁶ Surely he will never be shaken; the righteous will be in everlasting remembrance.

⁷ <u>He will not be afraid of evil tidings; his heart is steadfast, trusting in the LORD [YHVH].</u>

⁸ <u>His heart *is* established; he will not be afraid, until he sees *his desire* upon his enemies.</u>

What If Scriptures—Vol. 1

⁹ He has dispersed abroad, he has given to the poor; his righteousness endures forever; his horn will be exalted with honor.

¹⁰ The wicked will see *it* and be grieved; he will gnash his teeth and melt away; the desire of the wicked shall perish.

Psalm 115   <u>Not unto us, O LORD [YHVH], not unto us, but to Your name give glory, because of Your mercy, because of Your truth</u>.

² Why should the Gentiles say, "So where *is* their God?"

³ But our God *is* in heaven; He does whatever He pleases.

⁴ Their idols *are* silver and gold, the work of men's hands.

⁵ They have mouths, but they do not speak; eyes they have, but they do not see;

⁶ They have ears, but they do not hear; noses they have, but they do not smell;

⁷ They have hands, but they do not handle; feet they have, but they do not walk; nor do they mutter through their throat.

⁸ Those who make them are like them; *so is* everyone who trusts in them.

⁹ <u>O Israel, trust in the LORD [YHVH]; He *is* their help and their shield.</u>

¹⁰ <u>O house of Aaron, trust in the LORD [YHVH]; He *is* their help and their shield.</u>

¹¹ <u>You who fear the LORD [YHVH], trust in the LORD [YHVH]; He *is* their help and their shield.</u>

What If Scriptures—Vol. 1

¹² The LORD [YHVH] has been mindful of *us;* He will bless us; He will bless the house of Israel; He will bless the house of Aaron.
¹³ <u>He will bless those who fear the LORD [YHVH], *both* small and great.</u>
¹⁴ <u>May the LORD [YHVH] give you increase more and more, you and your children.</u>
¹⁵ <u>*May* you *be* blessed by the LORD [YHVH], who made heaven and earth.</u>
¹⁶ <u>The heaven, *even* the heavens, *are* the LORD's [YHVH'S]; but the earth He has given to the children of men.</u>
¹⁷ <u>The dead do not praise the LORD [Y-H], nor any who go down into silence.</u>
¹⁸ <u>But we will bless the LORD [Y-H] from this time forth and forevermore. Praise the LORD [Y-H]</u>!

Are you seeing this in your life?

What will it take for me to see this in my life?

What is the cost?

Even though things are getting worse, the LORD (YHVH) assured me He would protect those who fear and worship Him. That fear is not a reverential awe but more of a terror.

What If Scriptures—Vol. 1

What do you have to lose?

Grace and mercy are not for when we get it right, but for when we try and fail or come up short.

With God, the only way to lose is to quit trying.

What if you were that person in Psalm 112?

Psalm 2   Why do the nations rebel? Why are the countries devising plots that will fail?
2 The kings of the earth form a united front; the rulers collaborate against the Lord [YHVH] and his anointed king (Jesus).
3 They say, "Let's tear off the shackles they've put on us. Let's free ourselves from their ropes."
4 The one enthroned in heaven laughs in disgust; the Lord [YHVH] taunts them.
5 Then he angrily speaks to them and terrifies them in his rage, saying,
6 "I myself have installed my king [Jesus] on Zion, my holy hill."
7 <u>The king [Jesus] says, "I will announce the Lord's [YHVH's] decree. He said to me:</u>
'<u>You are my son. This very day I have become your father</u>.
8 Ask me, and I [YHVH] will give you the nations as your inheritance, the ends of the earth as your personal property.

What If Scriptures—Vol. 1

9 You will break them with an iron scepter; you will smash them like a potter's jar.'"
10 So now, you kings, do what is wise; you rulers of the earth, submit to correction.
11 Serve the Lord [YHVH] in fear. Repent in terror.
12 Give sincere homage. Otherwise he will be angry, and you will die because of your behavior,
when his anger quickly ignites. How blessed are all who take shelter in him! (NET)

In verse 7, it says, "This day I have become your father." What day is that? The day Jesus is installed as king or another? If there is a day when Jesus is declared a son, what was He before, if not a perfect man?

Psalm 102:12-22   But you, O LORD [YHVH], rule forever, and your reputation endures.
[13] You will rise up and have compassion on Zion. For it is time to have mercy on her, for the appointed time has come.
[14] Indeed, your servants take delight in her stones, and feel compassion for the dust of her ruins.
[15] The nations will respect the reputation of the LORD [YHVH], and all the kings of the earth will respect his splendor, [16] when the LORD [YHVH] rebuilds Zion, and reveals his splendor,

¹⁷ when he responds to the prayer of the destitute, and does not reject their request.
¹⁸ <u>The account of his intervention will be recorded for future generations; people yet to be born will praise the LORD [Y-H]</u>.
¹⁹ For he will look down from his sanctuary above; from heaven the LORD [YHVH] will look toward earth,
²⁰ in order to hear the painful cries of the prisoners, and to set free those condemned to die,
²¹ so they may proclaim the name of the LORD [YHVH] in Zion, and praise him in Jerusalem,
²² when the nations gather together, and the kingdoms pay tribute to the LORD [YHVH]. **(NET)**

Psalm 75   We give thanks to you, O God. We give thanks. You reveal your presence; people tell about your amazing deeds.
² <u>God says, "At the appointed times, I judge fairly</u>.
³ <u>When the earth and all its inhabitants dissolve in fear, I make its pillars secure." (Selah)</u>
⁴ I say to the proud, "Do not be proud,"
and to the wicked, "Do not be so confident of victory.
⁵ Do not be so certain you have won.
Do not speak with your head held so high.
⁶ For victory does not come from the east or west,
or from the wilderness. ⁷ <u>For God is the judge. He brings one down and exalts another</u>.

What If Scriptures—Vol. 1

⁸ For the LORD [YHVH] holds in his hand a cup full of foaming wine mixed with spices, and pours it out. Surely all the wicked of the earth will slurp it up and drink it to its very last drop."
⁹ As for me, I will continually tell what you have done; I will sing praises to the God of Jacob.
¹⁰God says, "I will bring down all the power of the wicked; the godly will be victorious." (NET)

Psalm 110   Here is the LORD's [YHVH'S] proclamation to my lord [Jesus]: "Sit down at my [YHVH's] right hand until I [YHVH] make your [Jesus'] enemies your [Jesus'] footstool."
² The LORD [YHVH] extends your [Jesus] dominion from Zion. Rule in the midst of your enemies.
³ Your people willingly follow you when you go into battle. On the holy hills at sunrise the dew of your youth belongs to you.
⁴ The LORD [YHVH] makes this promise on oath and will not revoke it: "You [Jesus] are an eternal priest after the pattern of Melchizedek."
⁵ O Lord [Jesus], at your right hand he strikes down kings in the day he unleashes his anger.
⁶ He executes judgment against the nations. He fills the valleys with corpses; he shatters their heads over the vast battlefield.

What If Scriptures—Vol. 1

[7] From the stream along the road he drinks; then he lifts up his head. (NET)

For these quotes, I have used the New English Translation (NET) of the Bible because I think it's clearer.

I have no idea what 110:7 means yet.

I think it is more than a coincidence that Psalms 2, 102, and 110 appear to refer to the millennial age. I also think it is more than coincidence that Psalm 102:18 says that a people yet to come will praise Y-H. From this it appears people will serve YHVH and praise Y-H.

What do you think?

CHAPTER 11

YHVH's Story

While I was working on this book, the Lord (YHVH) asked me to write His story. At first, I said "No" for fear of getting it wrong. After thinking about it and more discussion, I realized He knew the vessel and its issues and so I changed my decision. The only way I could write it was as a human being, communicating with other human beings. He said He was okay with that. Here is the story.

In the beginning, all I saw were math formulas. A correlation could be drawn to the movie "Matrix," where the perceived reality was overlaid by the program code executing, except there was no reality, just a kind of a pea soup green glow. I don't know how I knew the math symbols. It just made sense to me.

I became aware that off in the distance was a white light. How close or far, there was no way of knowing because there were no reference points, nothing.

With seemingly nothing to do, I studied the math. It appeared to emanate from the light and was

What If Scriptures—Vol. 1

everywhere. Some of the math pointed toward the light, some away, but most did neither. Eventually I became aware of a repeating pattern. What it was trying to portray, I didn't know. I determined that the answer had to be in the light because it was the source. The more intently I studied the light, the more frustrated I became as nothing was emerging. I decided to switch tactics and, instead of studying the light, I would allow the light to wash over me and experience its nuances.

There was peace and security in the light and something else that I couldn't quite figure out. This something else intrigued me. I began to repeat the math that was associated with this something else and began to let it direct me and carry me away.

It was then that I heard it—sound, something I had never experienced before. This was my first revelation. Each formula had a sound, and together they produced music.

I came to the conclusion that each grouping of sounds conveyed an idea. As I started to play the notes in my mind, I discovered that I had a voice. As I repeatedly sang the notes, an idea or revelation came to me. Eventually, I decoded the repeating patterns.

What If Scriptures—Vol. 1

It was saying, "I want offspring. Be fruitful, multiply, and have dominion."

What the extra something was, was purpose.

I don't know how I came into being. I only know that before me was nothing, and if I ever ceased to be, nothing would return. It was apparent whoever or whatever created me had a purpose for it and it wasn't hard to conclude that my existence was tied to the completion or fulfillment of that task. Because there was a lack of details, the only tools I had were the math formulas, it appeared as if the "how" was up to me. Soaking in the light brought no more revelation.

The first thought was, "Can I create an offspring by cloning myself?" That depended on the math of which I was composed. I studied myself and then sang the song. A ghostly form appeared before me, but it had no life. What was I missing? I tried it several more times with the same result.

I went back to the light and posed my question. As the light flooded over me, I saw the math dissolve, and a new math appeared that controlled the other math. There appeared to be no life in the math. Time after time, whatever I tried came up lifeless, although differing in extent of completeness. Maybe it was because I introduced slight inflections in my voice each time I sang. These inflections caused me to conclude that I was imperfect. The beauty of this imperfection was that it allowed for discovery in what I thought I knew. How amazing is my Creator!

I had to be asking the wrong questions. So, I asked "What question should I be asking?" What came back was, "Purpose without love is lifeless."

I had no concept of love. What did it mean? I thought about this for a while and decided I had a choice to make. How could I fulfill my purpose without love? Since I had already concluded that my existence was tied to the fulfillment of His purpose, I decided to go all in.

I asked, "Light me up with this love that is beyond the math, whatever it takes."

It started with a very soft melody, which was the most beautiful thing I had ever heard. Wave upon wave washed over me, changing me, activating me, until I became a reflection of the light and song. I became aware of the Spirit. While the math and sub-

What If Scriptures—Vol. 1

math gave me knowledge, the Spirit gave me truth and life. The concept of love had been born in me. I realized I was a new creation. While math showed me possibilities, this beyond-math love showed me possibilities with potential to fulfill the will of Him who was beyond the light.

I asked, "Light up the lifeless shells I created with Your love." There was no answer. Nothing.

"Why won't you do this? You did it for me." Nothing

I went back to allowing the light to wash over me. Nothing

Finally, I asked. "Love, what am I missing?"

Back came, "Who are you?"

I had contemplated *what* I was, but never *who*.

The Spirit of love prompted me, "I AM the first Son of the great I AM."

With this revelation, a massive amount of responsibility came flooding over me. This whole plan rested upon mé. It was overwhelming. If I could have run away, I would have. What was within me that gave Him confidence of my success? There appeared to be more to me than I knew. The Spirit of love said, "Trust Me, and I will give you the faith to accomplish all this and even more."

This utter dependence upon and submission to Him by choice was the basis of love, and the confidence that He would back His word to me with power and life gave me faith. I heard what was said, but I didn't know it.

The Spirit whispered, "Try it. Breathe life into your creation."

I breathed into one of the shells while saying, "What I have freely received, I freely give to you. Live!" Immediately it came to life. My first reaction was "Oh, my!"

This new life was just like what I had been, only knowing math. It was exciting teaching him to find his identity and the great command. However, I could only point him toward love. It had to be his choice.

What If Scriptures—Vol. 1

Before long, there were seven of them, basically all the same, but with subtle differences. It was then that the Spirit said, "Stop! You have enough."

I was before the group and said, "We are of the same basic formula, but each unique. How shall we be known? Who are we?"

One of the seven said, "What is the sound of our formula?"

"Beautiful," I thought and then I said, "We shall be known as the Elohiym."

The Spirit asked, "What is your unique name?"

I replied, "How can I select a name if I don't know the name of my Father beyond the light?"

The Spirit said, "What is the sound of love?"

We thought about this for a long time. We needed a sound that would convey awe, wonder, delight, sufficiency, infinity, and terror. We all agreed that the sound was "Ah!" However, as a name, we needed a way to define the sound that has no beginning or end. We all said, "His name is YAH."

What If Scriptures—Vol. 1

The Spirit said, "Amen!"

"Now that we know His name, my name shall be Yahweh or 'YAH exists' after the God I cannot see who exists beyond the light," I stated. Each one of them then selected a name pointing to our Father.

What we needed was a plan, but before that we needed to understand what we had. It was decided that two would catalog the math, two the sub-math, two would sing the math and sub-math songs, cataloging the results, and two would explore. I was one of the explorers.

We decided to start with the light because there was nothing else. As we went toward the light, there came a point where we could go no further. Here was a boundary. As we followed this boundary, we noticed a very slight curvature. We were inside a sphere. We went back to the light and tried different directions, all with the same curve. However, on one side of the light there was a bump, which turned out to be a fold. Within that fold, there was a crystal room full of light, and One in the room who was not like us.

"Who are you and what is this place?" I asked.

What If Scriptures—Vol. 1

He replied, "I am the Ancient of Days. I am here to keep a record of your progress, authorize and empower your plans, and judge the results."

"Have there been others before us?" I asked.

"Does it matter?" He said.

"I want to learn from prior failures. What, if any, advice can You give us?" I responded.

"As you have discerned," He said, "you are contained in a reality bubble. Therefore, contain your plans within their own bubbles. There are only two rules. 1). Never bring anyone or anything unholy into this realm, and 2). Don't quit fulfilling the great command you have been given. Succeed and eternal life beyond this realm is yours. Let me just say: you don't want to fail. Dominion also means discovery. There are very few limits. If you or your plans approach one, the Spirit will warn you. If you proceed, I will act, and it will not go well for all of you. My authority over you is absolute. I am the Protector of the Light."

We returned and called the group together, telling them what we had found and what was said. I joined those who were singing and cataloging. We changed our focus to find the math that generated a reality bubble.

Once the bubble was created, we focused on creating a gate by which we could enter and exit. We resumed singing the cataloged formulae inside the bubble, recording the results. There was almost an infinite combination of songs.

Every so often, we would convene and share ideas about how to use what we had learned to fulfill the great command. It wasn't until we discovered self-sustaining biological and chemical reactions that our plan started to develop. However, cross-contamination between different trials became a problem. It was decided to create sub-reality bubbles within the main test bubbles to isolate each test. Each one of us had his own sub-bubble to carry out testing. We agreed that sub-sub-reality bubbles were as far as we needed to go. If a test went awry, it was easy to delete the sub-bubble, to protect our other tests.

The cataloging of the formulae was finally complete. All of us were singing and cataloging the almost infinite combinations. We had regular meetings to compare testing results.

What If Scriptures—Vol. 1

One of us had the idea that he needed help managing his testing. He took our formula and de-tuned it to create a variety of helpers to manage the tests, including a host of creatures to manage the test environments. There were cherubim, seraphim, elders, archangels, angels, priests, and watchers, all embedded in the testing. When he related what he had done, it was such a blessing to us all that we decided to standardize on this method of test control.

We also decided we should have a singular primary test bubble. That way we could share the helpers. It was also decided that being the oldest, I would serve as lead in the group. Before we implemented this, we took it to the Ancient of Days for approval. His only requirement was that all the helpers and potential sons have free will. Free will is the ability to choose beyond what the math offers.

We divided the sub-test bubble into 24 sectors, with an elder responsible for each sector. Angels or messengers were established to keep the creatures contained and to carry out the desires of the Elohiym in charge. Archangels were there to keep any rebellions in check, oversee the angels, and ensure no outside forces interfered with the end game and timeline. Watchers would infiltrate the test to keep tabs on the creatures. Cherubim would be enforcers and constrainers, while seraphim would see the future for choices made.

After untold failures, it was decided that producing a perfect offspring wasn't possible. We always failed the "Love" test. Love had to come from within as a result of choice through submission to the Spirit and authority. It was not something we could engineer into a creature created by bio-chemical means. They would need a breath of the Spirit to give them the potential.

We decided to use imperfection as a way to develop a being capable of knowing love. Using imperfection meant that there would not be a 100% yield. Following numerous tests, vanity was the method for the highest quality yield. We determined quality versus quantity was vital in light of the warning of the Ancient of Day. In the same manner, there needed to be consequences for those failing.

The physical realm testing for the creation of bio-chem life was completed. But we had not completed cataloging all the possibilities. Two would continue cataloging while the rest developed this platform. There were numerous possibilities for creatures that

What If Scriptures—Vol. 1

had potential to fulfill the great command. These would be tested in unique bubbles, initially isolated from one another.

It was also apparent that this creating of offspring needed to be a multi-step process and not an event. Through more testing and discussion, a three-tiered set of reality bubbles appeared to give everything we needed to have a continuous process with maximum yield.

Again, we went back to the Ancient of Days for approval. He gave approval as long as all creation was subject to vanity. All Spirit-enabled beings whether helpers or prototypes were subject to the same limitations and consequences.

Once we knew that all our helper creatures needed to be subjected to vanity, the plan quickly took shape. We would create a beautiful creature that would succumb to his vanity and rebel. We would use this rebellion to create the choice necessary for the learning of love. This also meant that failure and restoration of the bio-chemical creature held the greatest potential for yield.

What If Scriptures—Vol. 1

The stage would be set by selecting a bio-chem creature and breathing into him the Spirit potential. By giving him authority, he would immediately become a target for the rebels. It would only be a matter of time until he gave in to them. This would happen because he did not know love.

This would accomplish two things: It would position the future son for ascension and position the rebels for decline. As he ascended, he would make the rebels his footstool. Love's two main components, mercy and grace, would be personified by my presence in a savior who would die for them. This choice was not a battle between good and evil, but rather a choice between math and the Spirit. (Fate [Life] or Love).

Math, even with all its possibilities, was ultimately deterministic and could never know love or have free will, especially when vanity was added to the equation. But the Spirit would allow for possibilities never allowed in math.

The truth was that the Spirit had the power to override the math. Only those who would choose the Spirit possibilities over what they could reason would be capable of understanding love, thereby becoming eligible for potential sonship. This choice could not be obvious and must be based upon seeking a relationship with the tests creator. This would be the first step in the process.

A side effect of using vanity was that the creature would worship what he feared. If he would fear an invisible God over tangible matter, he would have the potential, by being teachable, to become more than what the math dictated. If he could not overcome the fear of not being in control, he would not be a potential candidate. However, depending on his humility and faith, he might be useful as a servant elsewhere.

Each creature would be unique. Their success or failure would be determined by faith in the Spirit and what they did with what they were given individually.

Success would mean a realm in the second heaven called Paradise, where they would await completion of all things in the first heaven before continuing on. Failure was rewarded with a lake of fire in a special place in a realm.

The second step in the process would be their ability to demonstrate love, through humility, in the face of great temptations, trials, and arguments contrary to the Spirit's leading.

And thirdly, even though in authority, they would be willing to gladly die for their creatures possibilities.

While I was responsible for the entire plan, each of the Elohiym had their own section of the physical creation to oversee, along with the potential bio-chems of their choosing. As a way of limiting cross-contamination, initial bio-chem development would be conducted inside a reality bubble created through a rupture and singularity within a black hole.

Eligible prospects would graduate to the bigger universe outside the black hole and continue the great command to be fruitful, multiply, and have dominion while serving other step-one initiates to the glory of Him beyond the light as part of the second step of the process, finally serving as a host to his Elohiym, demonstrating mercy and grace and dying for another batch of potential sons before joining the Elohiym.

At any time, He who is beyond the light might take a son beyond the light.

What If Scriptures—Vol. 1

Our final plans were presented to the Ancient of Days, and He deliberated a long time before granting approval.

As Elohiym, we can see the end results of the math, but we cannot see the effects of the Spirit until the choice and resulting action of the Spirit-led being are complete. It is then that the hosts of Heaven are activated to make adjustments for the desired end game, timeline, and boundary enforcement.

In the beginning the Elohiym created the heavens and the earth, as the morning stars sang together.

That is the end of the story. I've included a picture for illustrative purposes only.

In the process of writing this, I had other inspirations and questions. These will be reserved for Volume 2.

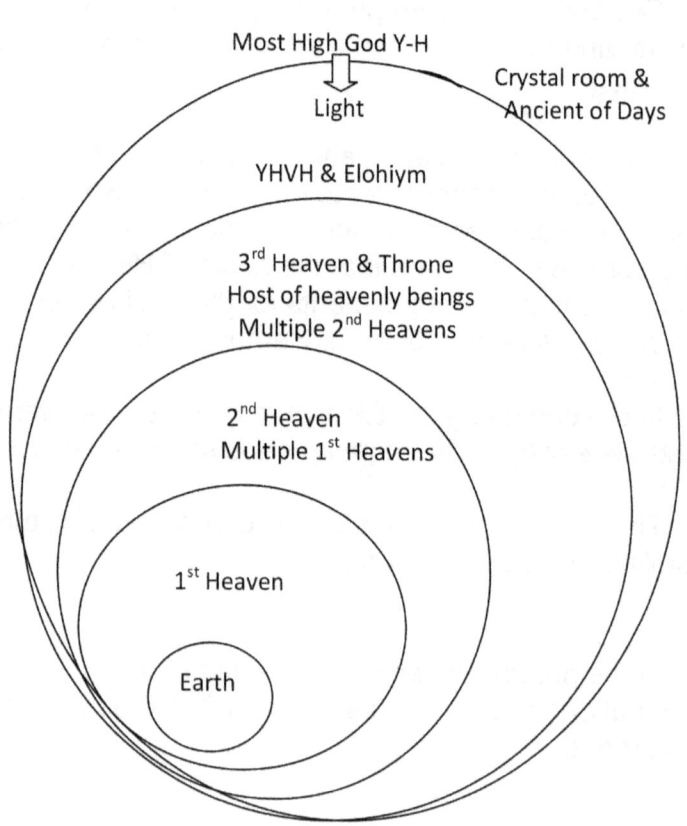

What If Scriptures—Vol. 1

This is my rendering of what was in the story. It was all I was given at the time.

What do you think?

SUMMARY

Let me just say that there are a lot more "What ifs" than we have been led to believe. If you believe there is only one interpretation of scripture, you are a grasshopper in the faith. If you believe yours is the only true interpretation, then you are deceived and don't know God. The scribes and Pharisees were this way, having one interpretation of scripture, but not knowing Him, and we know what Jesus said about them.

No matter where you are, you can always go deeper in God. Always leave yourself open to the possibility of more through the leading of the Holy Spirit.

You should always ask for two or three scriptures that validate what you think you heard the Holy Spirit saying. If you are not submitted to a human authority, <u>you will</u> go into a ditch. Share your revelations with your authority. Be aware that your "What Ifs" may bring the left foot of unfellowship.

Do not share your "What Ifs" with those who have no "What Ifs" of their own. 'What Ifs' that draw you away from God, His Spirit, His Word, the Church, or

What If Scriptures—Vol. 1

Christ are not His, although His may draw you away from a particular church.

My 'What Ifs' are mine. They are based on my perspectives, my experiences, and my relationship with God. Don't automatically buy into mine or anyone else's 'What Ifs.' God has some just for you. If this book has encouraged you to seek your own, then I have succeeded. *Seek ye first the kingdom of God and His righteousness…* Always be open to correction. If you cannot laugh at yourself, you really don't know God or what you are.

This is a living document, and as long as I am living, I will add or edit it as directed.

"The world has yet to see what God will do with a man fully consecrated to Him."
D. L. Moody

"Is there a limit to the possibilities for you in Him?"
T. R. Long

If you think the "Him" referenced multiple times above is Jesus, there are possibilities in Jesus, but so much more in Him. Jesus always pointed us to the Father.

What If Scriptures—Vol. 1

What do you think about these scriptures?

Psalm 91:9-10   Because you have made the LORD [YHVH], *who is* my refuge, *even* the Most High [Y-H?], your dwelling place, [10] No evil shall befall you, nor shall any plague come near your dwelling.

Isaiah 26:4   Trust in the LORD [YHVH) forever, for in JAH [Y-H] Jehovah [YHVH] *is* a Rock everlasting. (The Interlinear Bible)

Matthew 10:28   And do not fear those who kill the body but cannot kill the soul. But rather fear Him who is able to destroy both soul and body in hell.

James 1:17-18   Every good gift and every perfect gift is from above, and comes down from the Father of lights [Y-H], with whom there is no variation or shadow of turning. [18] Of His own will He brought us forth by the word of truth, that we might be a kind of firstfruits of His creatures.

Writing this book has changed me and my theology. I had no idea where this was headed when I started. I just had an unction to start.

What If Scriptures—Vol. 1

This doesn't mean that my previous understandings and revelations were wrong, but that in order to get a new understanding, I needed a new perspective. Those old understandings enabled me to get here.

The more I learn, the more I am in awe of the beauty of this creation and how little I think I know.

I have become more aware of my deficiencies and hidden sins. I thought I was clean, but what I needed was deep repentance. Repentance is a process, not an event.

This has been the hardest experience of my life, but I thank God for loving me through chastisement.

I have had to put things on the altar that I thought were part of my identity. I will be in this process until Jesus returns and it is completed.

While things around God and Jesus have changed for me, it is important to state some of the things that haven't changed.

1. The atoning blood of Jesus

> 2. There is no other name (Jesus) by which men can be saved
>
> 3. No one comes to the Father except through Jesus
>
> 4. Jesus is coming back to rule and reign
>
> 5. The sacraments are still intact
>
> 6. Numerous others…

The Spirit is saying loud and clear to all:

"Repent, for He is coming!"

Psalm 24:3-5   Who may ascend into the hill of the LORD [YHVH]?
Or who may stand in His holy place?
⁴He who has clean hands and a pure heart,
Who has not lifted up his soul to an idol,
Nor sworn deceitfully.
⁵He shall receive blessing from the LORD [YHVH],

What If Scriptures—Vol. 1

And righteousness from the God [Elohiym] of his salvation.

At the beginning of 2023, God told me, "Good things and bad things are coming. I will protect those who fear and worship Me!"

Be a dispenser of the love of God through His Spirit. The only way to get more is to give all you have in the service of the King.

The cover of this book is of the constellation Pleiades. Why are the constellations Pleiades and Orion mentioned together three times in the Old Testament? Pleiades is one of the smallest and Orion one of the largest. I hope to cover this in Volume 2.

Other books by Thomas R. Long available on Amazon.

The Gospel According to Tom

The Art of Standing

The Link

The Ultimate Simulation

www.ingramcontent.com/pod-product-compliance
Lightning Source LLC
LaVergne TN
LVHW092324080426
835508LV00039B/750